I Met
Jesus

I Met Jesus
when I was 14 years old

A testimony of meeting Jesus face to face.

Melanie Petrowski

Xulon Press

Xulon Press
555 Winderley Pl, Suite 225
Maitland, FL 32751
407.339.4217
www.xulonpress.com

© 2024 by Melanie Petrowski

Foreword by Ian Johnson

All rights reserved solely by the author. The author guarantees all contents are original and do not infringe upon the legal rights of any other person or work. No part of this book may be reproduced in any form without the permission of the author.

Due to the changing nature of the Internet, if there are any web addresses, links, or URLs included in this manuscript, these may have been altered and may no longer be accessible. The views and opinions shared in this book belong solely to the author and do not necessarily reflect those of the publisher. The publisher therefore disclaims responsibility for the views or opinions expressed within the work.

Unless otherwise indicated, Scripture quotations taken from the King James Version (KJV) – *public domain*.

Paperback ISBN-13: 979-8-86850-115-9
eBook ISBN-13: 979-8-86850-116-6

Dedication:

*This book is dedicated to Jesus Christ,
my Lord and Saviour,
the Bridegroom.*

Foreword

I first sat and talked with Melanie a number of years ago at a Church in Auckland and can remember listening to her testimony in the Church Cafe with my wife Joye. I was struck then by her powerful testimony. Her childlike faith that led to a face to face encounter with Jesus in an airport touched me deeply, as I too came to Jesus through a face to face encounter with Jesus.

Melanie lives life as someone who knows Jesus not just in an academic way, but as a personal friend, this comes through in this little book.

You will be impacted as you read, Jesus may not come to you in a leather coat in an airport, however He will come to you as you allow this testimony to stimulate your desire to know Him. He always meets people at the point of their desperation and need.

Revelation 12:11 speaks of the overcoming power of the blood of Jesus, and also the power of our testimony. The power of Melanie's testimony builds hope and faith in uncertain times.

I am happy to write the foreword to this book because it's an authentic real life testimony about Jesus and a young woman and the interactions they share on their journey together.

Ian Johnson
His Amazing Glory Ministries

Table of Contents:

1. The Seed of the Gospel 1
2. At Fourteen 5
3. The Significance of "Tree" 15
4. The Fire in His Eyes 21
5. I Wasn't Believed 25
6. The Revelation 27

Chapter 1.
The Seed of the Gospel

The seed of the gospel was sown back in 1982 when I was six years old at a primary (elementary) school called Mahora School, in Hastings, Hawke's Bay, New Zealand. I was in a regular, weekly class called Religious Education (or some called it Religious Instruction). I remember doing well and winning a prize, but I cannot recall exactly what we learnt. Obviously, it was about Jesus, God, and the Bible.

I wasn't brought up in a Christian home; all I was told by my mother was that I was baptised as a baby at the local Anglican church in Flaxmere, Hastings. From about six years old, I remember every night before I fell sleep, silently in my mind I would recite that little prayer, *"Now I lay me down to sleep, I pray the Lord my soul to keep, if I die before I wake, I pray the Lord my soul to take."*

One night, I was in bed lying on my belly, and my face was facing toward my left-hand side on a pillow. Suddenly, it felt like someone had sat on my bed beside me on my right-hand side; a presence. I froze and didn't want to look. I was scared. I didn't look. I didn't hear or feel anything physical or tangible, or I can't remember hearing or feeling anything physical or tangible, other than it felt like someone was sitting there on the bed. I can't recall exactly how long the feeling lasted; maybe it was only for a moment or a few minutes, and I can't recall if I drifted off to sleep right then and there or after the presence had gone. Was there a peace? I don't know. Maybe.

My parents were going through a divorce at that time. Even though my mother tried to make it work, there was still friction in the family home. Soon, maybe only days, after the first experience of feeling a presence or person sitting beside me while I was in bed, I felt another person or presence sitting on my bed in the same spot. Again, I was in the same position, lying on my belly with my head toward the left-hand side. And again, I froze and didn't look. This time, I heard a voice, not audible, but maybe within me, whispering to me in silence. It said, *"If you have to forgive, forgive the Devil."* And in my very young mind, I was like, "Ok, I forgive the Devil." It didn't really mean anything to me at the time, as I really didn't understand it. I was only six years old.

Weird and creepy things started happening in the home. Cockroaches were infesting the house, a peeping Tom started hanging around, and my parents finalised their divorce.

The Religious Education class carried on at primary school and into intermediate school, or middle school, up until I was twelve, and I enjoyed it very much. I remember having a lovely white Bible and hanging out with some Christian youth. I remember being scared when I was standing in the middle of a circle and the youth group were praying in tongues over me. I didn't understand it at the time, but after

I met Jesus when I was 14 years old

becoming a Christian, I realized they were blessing me, and I appreciate it now.

Chapter 2.

At Fourteen

Fast forward to when I was fourteen. I wondered about life and death and the purpose of life. I knew nobody was perfect, but that was a mystery to me, and I didn't know why or how to overcome that imperfection. Late at night on Thursday, August 16, 1990, I was lying in bed, pondering life and death. "Who am I? What am I?" I wondered. I felt to get out of bed, feeling compelled to kneel on the floor. I think The Holy Spirit drew me, but I didn't know it at the time. I dropped to my knees at the foot of my single bed with tears starting to roll down my face. I cried out to God as loud as I could from within me but without uttering a word. My mother was in the next room, and I didn't want her to hear me, nor did I want to wake her. I travailed silently for about three hours, and maybe a bit longer. Silently screaming, with my whole body braced and trembling, I ironically said to the Lord, "I do not know if You exist, God! I do not know if Jesus exists!"

I went into the bathroom and looked closely into the mirror, wondering, thinking, "Who am I? What am I? Why am I here?" All I could see was the little reflection of my face staring back at me through the small black pupils of my eyes. I could only see myself. Years later when I read the verse Deuteronomy 32:10 that said, *"He found him in a desert land, and in the waste howling wilderness; He led him about, He instructed him, He kept him as the apple of His eye,"* I remembered that instance and thought, "Oh, maybe when I saw myself in my own eye, God was showing me that I was the apple of His eye?"

After reading that whole verse, I believe that's what God was doing with me. He found me in the desert place of my life, the literal waste howling wilderness of my soul. He led me to the floor, and He and His Holy Spirit led and instructed me to pray and travail, and He showed me I was the apple of His eye. He has kept me the apple of His eye ever since.

I only spent a few minutes in the bathroom staring into the mirror, thinking hard about my dilemma, wondering who I was, then I went back to bed. But I didn't sleep very well, as the crying and travailing throughout the night exhausted me.

After not sleeping very well or for very long, the next day, I had to get up early and get ready for my second day of work experience out at the small local, domestic airport, Napier Airport. My high school, Hastings Girls' High School, organised a work experience week in the local area. I wanted to be a flight attendant, so weeks prior, arrangements were made through my high school to go to a local travel agent for the first three days of the week and out to the airport for two days. My mother had arranged for her friend's husband, who was a courier driver and regularly drove out to the airport, to pick me up.

The day before, on my first day volunteering at the airport, I was ready to go on time. I was all prim and proper, looking very professional with make-up on and everything. But this day was very different. I was all dishevelled with no make-up on, looking drained and tired from all the travailing and crying out to the Lord. The courier driver was taken aback when I opened the front door to him. He literally stepped back in surprise. "Oh well, not to worry," I thought. I took my make-up bag with me.

When I got to the airport, I popped into the women's bathroom to apply my makeup. Afterward, I was all ready to go and feeling good. I went behind the long white check-in counter, but no planes were coming in or going out, not arriving or departing, at that particular time. Then, a man of average height, with bright red hair and strikingly bright blue eyes, approached me at the counter. I don't really know what possessed me to do what I did, maybe it was the Holy Spirit, but I leaned over the counter, looked him right in the eyes, and I asked him, "Are you…?"

He stopped me right there and said, "No, but He's walking in now." I don't know why, but I was going to ask him, "Are you Jesus?" For some reason, he knew what I was going to say. I asked him for his name and he told me, "Mr Fisher." Years later, after pondering this experience, I wondered who that could've been. Was he Jesus's disciple, Peter? He was a fisherman. Was he Gabriel? He heralded the Lord's presence. Fisher is a very interesting name, as we are all called to be "fishers of men," so maybe it was meant to be humorous? I'm sure God will tell me when the time comes.

No word of a lie, on Friday, August 17, 1990, Jesus Christ in the flesh walked into this little local, regional airport on this little island, in this little country at the ends of the earth. He didn't walk straight up to me. He walked straight ahead inside the main doors to the left of me, down the centre aisle, and between the two sets of seats, containing about five rows of about ten seats each. He sat down in the front row on the righthand side, a few seats in from the aisle, looking out of the big airport window toward the empty tarmac.

I started crying from behind the counter. *There goes the make-up.* I came out from around the counter and started walking passed Mr Fisher and toward Jesus, Who was still sitting in the front row, looking out to the tarmac. I thought I should introduce myself since that's what you do when you meet someone new. I stood in front of Him as He sat there. He looked at me. I said, "Hi, my name is—"

"I know who you are," He interrupted. Years later I realised it was like introducing myself to my parents. He created me! Of course He knew who I was. I was very nonchalant and thought, *"Ok"* and sat down next to Jesus on the right of Him. I instinctively knew that He knew everything.

I had always wondered about aliens, so I asked Jesus, "Do other life forms exist?"

He said, "Yes." Again, I was very nonchalant and did not ask Him to expound or elaborate on His answer. Later, I wondered if He meant angels and demons by "other life forms," as there was a time where I thought maybe aliens didn't exist, as many Christians don't believe they do. But as time went by, many people, including Christian Bible scholars, have said aliens do exist, and many others, including pilots, have had experiences with aliens. So I now think they *do* exist, but that's a whole other book.

Jesus never introduced Himself or even hinted to who He was. He was very handsome, with green-blue eyes, wavy shoulder length brown hair that was parted in the middle, and olivey tanned skin. He wore clothes for that day, layered with a long leather coat. He had gloves on, as I assume He did not want me to see the holes in His hands and wrists. He said to me, "I'm married!"

In the far background behind Him, near the other set of seats, was a Japanese-looking lady, who was watching us. "Are you married to that lady?" I innocently and ignorantly responded.

He chuckled and said, "No, read the Bible."

"But isn't the Bible misinterpreted?" I replied.

He looked at me, frowning, as if to be sad about it, and said, "Yes, but…" He paused, allowing me to finish the sentence.

"But it's true," I said.

"Yes," He answered.

So, *the Bible is true.*

I asked Jesus if the lady in the background was Japanese, and He nodded yes. I thought I could impress her with my Japanese language, as I had been learning it at high school. I walked over to her, and I attempted to introduce myself in Japanese. "*Konichi wa, watashi no namae wa Merani desu,*" which translates to, "Hello, my name is Melanie."

She smiled and nodded but didn't talk to me or tell me her name. She was tall and beautiful. She could have been an angel or a distant relative of mine whom Jesus allowed to return to earth to visit me. Or, she could've been the person of the Holy Spirit. I don't actually know who she was, and Jesus didn't tell me, nor did I ask. I turned, looking out the large window passed the tarmac and toward the hills in the far distance, and all I could think of was *"ki"* for tree. So I pointed out toward the trees and said *"Ki!"* Again, she just smiled and nodded. She was probably laughing at me on the inside. It was like God had blocked my mind for any other words. Years later, I realised that maybe God wanted me to only know "tree" because it is important and relevant in so many ways.

Chapter 3.
The Significance of "Tree"

Again, years later, after pondering upon "tree" and looking it up in the Bible, I discovered many significant meanings and reasons behind "tree." These scriptures are really good for us to know, and for us to understand how they relate to Jesus and us.

- Jesus died on a tree—the cross of Christ was made of wood from a tree (Mat. 27:40, Mark 15:32, Luke 23:26, John 19:17).

- Jesus is the Tree of Life (Gen. 2:9 [though it doesn't specifically say it, Jesus is the Way, the Truth, and the Life – John 14:6, and Jesus is the Resurrection and the Life – John 11:25]).

- The kingdom of Heaven and the kingdom of God, which is within us (Luke 17:21), is like a tree—it starts off as small as a mustard seed and grows into a tree (Mat. 13:32, Luke 13:18-19).

- The tree of the field is man's life (Deu. 20:19).

- Wisdom is a tree of life (Pro. 3:18).

- The fruit of the righteous is also a tree of life (Pro. 11:30), and the righteous shall flourish as a branch (Pro. 11:28).

- A wholesome tongue is a tree of life (Pro. 15:4).

- We are trees—a good tree brings forth good fruit, and a corrupt tree, bad fruit. If we don't bring forth good fruit, we will be cut down and cast into the fire (Mat. 3:10, 7:17; Luke 3:9, 6:43).

- We are like trees planted by water, grounded in the Word of the Lord, whose leaves always stay green (spiritually healthy) and will bear fruit (Jer. 17:8).

- Because Zacchaeus climbed a sycamore tree to see Jesus (Luke 19:2-4), it has somewhat become a symbol of clarity.

- The Book of Revelation mentions the tree of life, which is *"in the midst of the paradise of God,"* and which *"bare twelve manner of fruits, and the leaves of the tree were for the healing of the nations"* and *"blessed are they that do his commandments, that they may have the right to the tree of life"* (Rev. 2:7, 22:2, 14).

- Jesus also speaks of trees when talking about His return.

Luke 21:27-31 reads:

> *^{27} And then shall they see the Son of man coming in a cloud with power and great glory.*

²⁸ And when these things begin to come to pass, then look up, and lift up your heads; for your redemption draweth nigh.

²⁹ And he spake to them a parable; Behold the fig tree, and all the trees;

³⁰ When they now shoot forth, ye see and know of your own selves that summer is now nigh at hand.

³¹ So likewise ye, when ye see these things come to pass, know ye that the kingdom of God is nigh at hand.

- He is the Branch, and the Vine, and we are His branches too (Zec. 6:12, John 15:1-2).

- People also took branches from palm trees and laid them down in front of Jesus, riding into Jerusalem, singing *"Hosanna: Blessed is the King of Israel that cometh in the name of the Lord"* (*John 12:13, Mark 11:8*). A palm branch is a symbol of triumph, peace, and eternal life and represents victory of the spirit over the flesh (Rev. 7:9).

A more extensive study of verses that mention branches and vines can be found in the books of Isaiah, Jeremiah, Luke, John, and Romans.

I went and sat down next to Jesus again and asked Him, "Where are you going today?"

And guess what He said? "Christchurch."

I was again nonchalant and said, "Ok," but years after, I had to chuckle. Get it? Christ-church—Christ's church! God has a sense of humour! Or, He could've actually been on His way to Christchurch, which is a city in the South Island of New Zealand (and other places around the world), but I'm sure He was playing with words. He likes to do that, I've discovered. Jesus is funny!

Chapter 4.

The Fire in His Eyes

I looked down and thought, "I'm in love with this man. If only I look at Him in His eyes, He might fall in love with me too." So I looked up into His eyes, and I saw flames of fire in His eyes! I literally saw the flames of fire in His eyes as described in Daniel 10:6 and Revelation 2:18:

> *His body also was like the beryl, and his face as the appearance of lightning, and his eyes as lamps of fire, and his arms and his feet like in colour to polished brass, and the voice of his words like the voice of a multitude. (Daniel 10:6)*
>
> *And unto the angel of the church in Thyatira write; These things saith the*

> *Son of God, who hath his eyes like unto a flame of fire, and his feet are like fine brass.* (Revelation 2:18)

Suddenly, it was like I saw or knew my future sin in my mind, and I felt kind of ashamed. I looked down in shame. He was so pure and holy.

I suddenly had a vision or thought of Jesus being scourged and tortured, and I started crying. He consoled me by putting His right arm around my shoulders. I felt peace. I think He knew what I was seeing in my mind. I think He put what I was seeing in my mind. He took my shame and died for my sins (and yours), including my future sin that I saw just before.

He already loves us very much. He doesn't need us to convince Him to love us like I thought in my little fourteen-year-old head. He already took the torture for us. God has already forgiven us because of that scourging and torture on His Son, Jesus. We just have to open up our hearts to Him and say yes to His love. It's like the most perfect, amazing, wise, loving, strong, and gentle man is asking us to marry Him. We just have to say "yes!"

I looked around the airport because I thought that if the staff saw me talking to a "passenger" and crying, they may freak out and think I'm weird or judge my behaviour, thinking it was kind of like misconduct or unprofessional to disrupt a passenger, let alone cry on His shoulder. But no one was around. No passengers, not even the staff. It was like time had stood still. There was still no planes going in or out. It was like we were in a time bubble in another dimension, but it was real life, and we were on Earth.

The next thing I knew, Jesus was walking toward the main doors to exit, now dressed in white, and I was near the check-in counter a few feet away. As I watched Him walk away, I thought in my mind, *"Now if you really are Jesus, you'd turn around and look at me,"* and He did! He didn't say a thing, just turned and looked at me for a moment and then turned back around and started walking again. I thought, *"Ok, if you really REALLY are Jesus, you'd turn around and look at me again,"* but He didn't, as He had already proven Himself once, and maybe, I guess, I was tempting God. Or maybe Jesus had a smile on His face and chuckled as He walked away and thought I was just being silly.

The whole experience felt like about twenty minutes, but it could've been minutes or even seconds or hours. Who knows? I think I went back into the bathroom to sort my make-up out again, and once I came out, I went back behind the check-in counter. Staff came out, and passengers started entering and checking in, and a plane landed.

Chapter 5.
I Wasn't Believed

I told my mum that night, but she didn't believe me and thought I was crazy. She even got her sister, my aunty, around to talk to me. I remember her putting her hands around my face and saying, "You're a beautiful girl. You don't have to think like this." I felt a strong, tangible presence of the Holy Spirit around me for about three days afterward. Even my cat could sense something, as he was always looking at me—no, staring at me—and acting weird around me. I don't think I told anyone that story again till at least twenty years later.

And my journey continued, but that's for another time.

Chapter 6.

The Revelation

Now, though years later, I had a revelation that the airport seats were set up like they would be in a church for a wedding, with rows of seats and an aisle in the middle. Jesus walked "down the aisle" and not around to where I was standing behind the counter. He sat down in the front row on the right-hand side, which is a place of honour, as described in Hebrews 1:3, 12:2, 1 Peter 3:22, Acts 7:55-56. He was somewhat like a Bridegroom, waiting for His bride. No wonder He told me He was married! I discovered He is married to the church. And we, who are all those who say yes to Jesus, are His bride, His church! It's that simple. Jesus is asking us, the whole world, to be part of His bride, His church. He did, after all, die for the whole world:

> "For God so loved the world, that he gave his only begotten Son, that whosoever believeth in him should not perish, but have everlasting life" (John 3:16).

Jesus calls Himself the Bridegroom, and there are many Bible verses that mention the "bridegroom."

> Matthew 9:15
> *And Jesus said unto them, can the children of the bridechamber mourn, as long as the bridegroom is with them? But the days will come, when the bridegroom shall be taken from them, and then shall they fast.*

> Luke 5:34-35
> *And he said unto them, Can ye make the children of the bridechamber fast, while the bridegroom is with them? But the days will come, when the bridegroom shall be taken away from them, and then shall they fast in those days.*

Mark 2:19-20
And Jesus said unto them, can the children of the bridechamber fast, while the bridegroom is with them? As long as they have the bridegroom with them, they cannot fast.

But the days will come, when the bridegroom shall be taken away from them, and then shall they fast in those days.

Isaiah 61:10
I will greatly rejoice in the Lord, my soul shall be joyful in my God; for he hath clothed me with the garments of salvation, he hath covered me with the robe of righteousness, as a bridegroom decketh himself with ornaments, and as a bride adorneth herself with her jewels.

Isaiah 62:5b
…and as the bridegroom rejoiceth over the bride, so shall thy God rejoice over thee.

Jeremiah 33:11
The voice of joy, and the voice of gladness, the voice of the bridegroom, and the voice of the bride, the voice of them that shall say, Praise the Lord of hosts: for the Lord is good; for his mercy endureth for ever: and of them that shall bring the sacrifice of praise into the house of the Lord. For I will cause to return the captivity of the land, as at the first, saith the Lord.

Joel 2:16
Gather the people, sanctify the congregation, assemble the elders, gather the children, and those that suck the breasts: let the bridegroom go forth of his chamber, and the bride out of her closet.

Matthew 25:1
Then shall the kingdom of heaven be likened unto ten virgins, which took their lamps, and went forth to meet the bridegroom.

Matthew 25:6
And at midnight there was a cry made, Behold, the bridegroom cometh; go ye out to meet him.

Matthew 25:10
And while they went to buy, the bridegroom came; and they that were ready went in with him to the marriage: and the door was shut.

John 3:29
He that hath the bride is the bridegroom: but the friend of the bridegroom, which standeth and heareth him, rejoiceth greatly because of the bridegroom's voice: this my (John the Baptist's) joy therefore is fulfilled.

Jesus wants a relationship with us, to commit to us, and for us to commit to Him. In fact, Jesus is asking us to marry Him and be part of His bride, which is His church. Will you say "yes" to Jesus? And it's ok for males to be part of the Bride of Christ, just as it's ok for females to be part of mankind. Please, say *yes* to Jesus; it'll be the best decision you ever make.

I hope you've found this story of my experience meeting Jesus face to face insightful and revelatory. If you ever find yourself travailing and crying out to God, may the Lord bless you also with an unforgettable experience with our Lord Jesus Christ. He loves you with an everlasting love.

Milton Keynes UK
Ingram Content Group UK Ltd.
UKHW031951281024
450365UK00008B/402